P9-CRM-562

JEWELS
FOR A CROWN

The Story
of the
Chagall Windows

ותורתך

MIRIAM FREUND

JEWELS *for* A CROWN

The Story of the Chagall Windows

FOREWORD BY

RENÉ D'HARNONCOURT

DIRECTOR, MUSEUM OF MODERN ART, NEW YORK

Illustrated
with 13 plates in 6 colors

McGRAW-HILL BOOK COMPANY, INC.
NEW YORK TORONTO LONDON

TO GILEAD AND REBECCA CARMEL

MY THANKS TO RUTH GRUBER FOR HER INVALUABLE HELP IN THE PREPARATION OF THE TEXT FOR THIS BOOK.

Library of Congress Catalog Card Number : 63-19440
22320

PRINTED IN FRANCE
BY IMPRIMERIE NATIONALE AND IMPRIMERIE DU LION

FOREWORD

MARC CHAGALL'S famed Jerusalem Windows were commissioned by Hadassah for the synagogue of its Hebrew University Medical Center. They are the latest and most monumental of his many works which take subject matter and inspiration from the Scriptures.

As early as 1931 the artist visited Egypt, Syria and Palestine to see with his own eyes the setting for the Bible illustrations that were to occupy much of his time until the outbreak of the Second World War. In these engravings and in many drawings and paintings the artist treated his Biblical subjects with a passion and reverence that reflected the mystic folklore of the Jewish community in his native town of Vitebsk.

Most of these earlier works illustrated specific incidents and situations, but in the Jerusalem Windows Chagall selected a much broader theme : the twelve tribes of Israel and the twelve sons of Jacob from whom the tribes were descended. In order to weld together this vast subject Chagall resorted to the use of symbols brought to life by the artist's passion and the craftsman's skill. That he succeeded in his task became evident even before the installation of the windows in Israel. The previews given the Jerusalem Windows in Paris and New York were received with great enthusiasm by extraordinarily large audiences.

The book is particularly dedicated to young people, but it also aims to bring the message of Chagall's work to all those who have not been able to see the originals and to those who want to relive the experience of seeing them. It is eminently fitting that it should have been prepared by Dr. Miriam Freund, who has already done so much to make them accessible to the American public.

RENÉ D'HARNONCOURT

May, 1963

Marc Chagall, the great French painter, suddenly left his easel and knelt down on the floor and began to throw odd-shaped bits of colored cloth, papers and other materials onto a large white sheet of paper. Then he became absorbed in moving the bits of paper and cloth around. His wife Vava, who had been standing in the doorway watching him, burst out, "What are you doing, Marc?"

"I have decided to make the designs for the windows of a house of worship in the hills of Judea. Do you remember the visitors from America who came to see us some weeks ago? They told us about a new medical center they were building in Jerusalem."

"Oh yes, the President of Hadassah and their architect!"

"Well, I have been thinking about the talk we had and their request that I work with them. I keep remembering that they said, "'We are asking this not only for Hadassah but for the Jewish people too.'" I haven't been able to sleep.

I keep seeing that small jewel of a synagogue they described and I want to make a beautiful crown for it, a jeweled crown of twelve stained-glass windows. Windows which will catch the light of the air of Jerusalem and reflect it in a thousand, thousand colors. I feel I can do it! I feel I must do it!"

Thus began the story of these famous Chagall Windows. No, not began, really, because for its true beginning we have to go back, far back, to the year 1887 when a baby boy, Marc, was born to Mama Chagall in the Russian town of Vitebsk (pronounced Vee/tepsk). Marc grew to boyhood in that town and he never forgot its smells, its sights, its tastes – memories of it have constantly shaped his life and his work.

Chagall himself has taught us to go back to that childhood to understand him, for he says over and over again that all his work is a kind of yearning for his mother and father and Vitebsk. "My father and my mother were my first museum, my first Louvre, my first Hermitage..."

The Bible was the first book Marc Chagall studied as a boy in Vitebsk, and it remained the most important book in his life. The miracles in the Bible were all real to little Marc, so real that they stopped being miracles. As he read the Bible he could see the Red Sea opening for Moses. He knew how Abraham was about to sacrifice little Isaac on the mountain and was stopped by the Angel. He learned of the blessings that Jacob, who is Israel, gave his sons on his deathbed.

In 1931, he made his first visit to the countries of the Bible and traveled in Egypt, Syria and the land of Israel. He understood and repeated what the Sages had said: "The air of the Land of Israel makes one wise." As he walked in the very fields where Jacob and his sons had walked, breathed the air of Jerusalem and saw the valleys where the great heroes and the prophets of the Bible had lived, the Bible was with him as guide and friend. He wrote then, "In the East, I unexpectedly found the Bible and a part of my very being."

Although he had passed his seventy-second birthday, he was like a joyous child that day in his studio, talking to his beloved Vava, planning the crown of twelve stained-glass windows. Though no one had told him what to put in his windows, it was all there in his mind, shaped by his memories and the Bible. Twelve windows! Twelve sons of Jacob! Twelve tribes of Israel!

As he worked at his easel, in his studio in Vence in southern France, he forgot that the hills of Provence were outside his windows. He was in the land of Canaan sitting in the tent of Jacob. He came to know the house of Jacob as if it were his own, and each son as if he were his own – especially the two favorite sons, born of Rachel. Young Joseph in his coat of many colors and little Benjamin, the baby!

He stood at the bedside of the dying Jacob, who, when he was a hundred and forty-seven years old, called his twelve sons to bless them. "Gather yourselves together; and hear ye, sons of Jacob; and hearken unto Israel, your father."

Thus Jacob spoke to his twelve sons and gave his blessings – to each according to his merit. Jacob knew his boys very well; their faults and their virtues; their weaknesses and their strengths.

Chagall lovingly repeated the words of each blessing found in Genesis 49 until he knew them by heart. He remembered too the blessings of Moses (Deuteronomy 33), who, on his deathbed blessed the twelve tribes, descendants of the sons of Jacob.

Chagall knew the Hebraic tradition that paintings of human beings may not be used in a synagogue. Thus he could not paint portraits of Joseph or Benjamin or Reuben on his windows, but he could and would paint animals and fish and flowers. Lions and birds and gay little crooked houses, with the radiant sun and the blue-green sea, would flow across his windows. And out of all that would come fire and radiance and a great harmony.

Now began many months of work! There were five steps in making the designs which preceded the actual work on the glass. First, Chagall drew sketches in pen and pencil and India ink. Then came a preparatory drawing, again in

India ink and wash, in which he blocked in the general outlines for the window – a little wolf in the lower left corner, a donkey at the top, sitting above the small circles swirling like planets in the large circle that could be the universe.

Then he decided what the basic color for each window should be. In Benjamin, for example, one of the most beautiful and inspired of all the windows, he decided the background color should be blue, and so he now had to work out the relationship of colors and shapes to the basic background color. In this fourth step, he made a small model in gouache and collage. He collected bits and pieces of colored fabrics and colored papers, bits of grass and colored glass, and threw them all into a large sheet of paper. He had the purple blue of the night sky, the blue-green of grass, the sun-spattered blue of the Mediterranean – but there were also pieces in shades of yellow, green, mauve, violet and purple. As he worked with these colors, a subtle blending of form and color emerged – and Chagall was ready for the fifth step and the final model.

This final stage was the finished design called the *maquette,* (pronounced ma-ket). Using water colors which he mixed as he worked, he painted in the blue background and followed the colors of the collage. The colors themselves and their shape gave new flight to his imagination. In a triangle of yellow that he had placed next to the purple wolf, he painted in swift black strokes the two cities he loves – Vitebsk with its crooked little houses and Jerusalem with its minarets and the Tower of David. There were twelve maquettes, one for each of the twelve windows, and he worked and reworked each one until it said in its own mysterious way what Chagall felt.

From the earliest rough sketches to the final designs there were many months of hard work. But this was only the first stage. The designs now had to be transferred to glass.

Chagall took the maquettes to the ancient cathedral town of Reims, eighty-five miles northeast of Paris, and there he entered into a partnership with two young artists, Charles and Brigitte Simon-Marq. The Marqs own and manage one of the oldest and most famous stained-glass *ateliers* or workshops in France. In this workshop, the Jacques Simon Atelier, generation after generation of fathers and sons have been making stained-glass windows for the cathedrals of the world since the sixteenth century. In our time, the secret of their great art has been passed from Jacques Simon to his daughter Brigitte and to her husband Charles Marq. Charles and Brigitte had worked with Chagall on his windows for the Metz Cathedral, and they were excited by this new commission.

They began to work with the glass itself. Chagall loves the word glass. He calls the windows his "glasses." For him, stained glass is a more exciting challenge than painting on a flat canvas, because glass has movement and life. It is made of pure sand called silica – and a great deal of it is found in Israel in the very desert where Jacob and his sons lived. This fine white sand is mixed with lime and soda and heated until it melts. Then it is called "molten glass." Molten glass can be rolled like pastry dough, and it can even be spun and woven and blown. For glass is really a liquid which has become solid and can easily become liquid again.

Chagall and his two young friends went to the St. Juste Glass Works in the Loire Valley, where special glass was made for them. Sheets of glass of more than fifty colors were blown and rolled. Pigments were mixed together to get the brilliant colors that Chagall wanted, some of them as fresh and iridescent as jewels, some as soft as a baby's blanket or the fleece of a lamb.

In the glass factory they used many methods to get the colors and shades of color into the glass itself – those colors that Chagall had painted on his paper in his studio. Sometimes they tried techniques that had been used in the Middle Ages and then forgotten. Sometimes they worked out new techniques that nobody had ever used before.

If they wanted to get a special tone of brilliant red, for

instance, Charles Marq would choose a piece of red glass. While this red glass was burning hot and liquid, like a flowing river of red, a worker blew it into the shape of a little balloon. He dipped this hot red balloon into clear glass or glass that was slightly tinted. This glass too was hot and liquid. With the little red balloon inside the clear glass, he continued blowing until he had a large balloon, with red glass inside and clear glass outside. Then he flattened the big balloon and rolled it until it was a single sheet of glass.

Now he had the tone of stained glass that he wanted – with a thin layer of red glass laminated onto a thicker bottom layer of clear or faintly tinted glass.

It was this unique method of getting different shades of color which makes the windows seem to curve and makes some of the designs seem to come startingly forward as if they stand right out of the windows, while other designs seem to move back and recede gently into the background. It is usually the reds that come forward and the blues and greens that move away from the eye as the sun pours through the different depths of color.

Because the Jerusalem sun seems to be like no other sun in the world, especially as it begins to set in golden hues coloring the stones of the Hills of Judea, Charles and Brigitte Marq traveled to Jerusalem to study the light as it filtered through colored glass. They took with them four sample panels in the four dominant colors – blue, red, yellow and green. They spent hours watching the light change as the sun rose into the sky and then descended as the day grew long and darkness began to fall. They worked out plans for how thick or thin to make the top layer of color so that the light could come through and create the desired tone. For this is the key to making stained glass – to keep the color layer thin enough so that light can come through.

Once the problem of the colored sheets of glass was settled, the Marqs returned to the atelier, where large black-and-white photographs were made of Chagall's twelve maquettes. Each photograph was placed on a table whose top was translucent glass. An electric bulb underneath the table lit up the photograph. The photograph was the exact size that the finished window would be – approximately eleven feet high and eight feet wide, and curved on top to fit inside an arched frame.

On the table, the photograph was traced on white transparent paper, with black lines to show where the lead would be placed around the pieces of colored glass.

Each piece inside its lead frame was numbered; each piece was then traced on heavy brown paper, and each numbered piece of brown paper was cut out. The pieces of brown paper were like patterns for a dress. They were the patterns, in the exact size and shape, for the individual pieces of glass.

Now the glass was brought in. The pieces of brown paper were placed above the layer of colored glass that matched Chagall's colors in the maquettes. The shapes of the glass were cut by skilled craftsmen with a special glass cutter with a diamond point. In order to make some of the glass thinner than the rest and to give it a different color value, Marq devised a brand new technique. He played a thin stream of acid on the colored glass. With quick brush strokes, he moved the few drops of acid across the surface of the glass. This could cloud or lighten the color, or reduce the thickness of the glass, or create bubbles in the glass. By this process, when the outer layer is "bitten" by the acid, its color tones are modified by those of the layer below.

A great artist in glass, Charles Marq was able to get three or four or even more different shades of single color into a single cut-out piece of glass.

Now the small pieces of glass were fitted together, almost like the pieces of a jig-saw puzzle. They were placed into grooved strips of lead so that the glass could slide in easily. Charles Marq didn't want the lead to cut through the birds and fish and flowers and geometric designs, so frequently he drew the lead right into the design. Sometimes a strip of lead might become the body of a fish or the beak of a bird or an eye that looks almost human.

Sometimes the lead was worked in a geometric pattern or in circles; sometimes it seems to curve and flow across the window. The entire window is then divided into twelve sections of copper framework, which hold together the dozens of little pieces of stained glass, each in its own grooved lead stripping.

This is called the "first assemblage." But it is still a "dead window." The "living window" is yet to come.

The assembled window in its strong copper framing was hung on a wall in the atelier. Chagall, standing on a ladder, began to paint in *grisaille* (a gray color that varies from light to dark) on the colored glass itself. He was making what he calls an "*echt* Chagall," a real Chagall. He was putting his own touches in – the marks of Chagall. Through his use of grisaille, he regulated the transparency, strengthened certain areas and gave rhythm and life. This took time, much effort and great patience.

Chagall has said a work of art should have "the freshness and naturalness of a child, it should be full of love – like a child. Warmth, love – this is the most important thing in art."

As he finished putting the "Chagall touch" on each window, it was taken down and disassembled. Now each piece of glass was fired in the oven, so the fire would keep Chagall's touch of genius upon the glass forever.

Then came the "second assemblage." All the pieces were fitted into their places, securely held in their thick strips of lead and their large copper framework. Chagall stood back and looked at his window.

Now, at last, it was "living glass." This process was repeated for each one of the twelve windows. But before they could be shipped to Israel for installation in the Jerusalem Synagogue, the French Museum came to Chagall and asked that his "glasses" be exhibited in Paris. Chagall was honored, and agreed. The government built a special pavilion for the windows in the Jardin des Tuileries of the Louvre Museum in Paris. It was the highest honor they could give a living artist. Critics said, "The windows are Chagall's masterpiece."

The American women's organization, Hadassah, which had commissioned the windows, wanted America to see the windows, too. They arranged with the Museum of Modern Art in New York to exhibit the windows. Once again, each piece of glass was taken out of its lead frame, packed as carefully as an egg and as tenderly as a flower, and each of the twelve windows was flown in its own box to New York.

Nearly a quarter of a million people came to look at the "glasses." In homes all over New York, there was an excited return to reading the Bible.

Critics said the windows were among the greatest achievements of twentieth-century art. Some said they were among the greatest examples of stained-glass art of all time, including the great days of the Middle Ages.

Now the windows were taken down once again, but this time they were flown to Israel – to the synagogue set into the Hills of Judea.

The windows are arranged there just the way the tribes of Israel grouped themselves in the desert to protect the Holy Ark as they journeyed to the Promised Land. They made four human walls around the Ark, with three tribes forming each wall.

It was a sunny day in February, 1962, when the windows came home. Marc Chagall came from France with his wife Vava. Charles and Brigitte Marq had come weeks before to make sure the windows were installed correctly. High officials of Israel and Hadassah came for the dedication ceremonies. There were many speeches.

But it was Chagall's words that remain as a blessing forever.

"How is it that the air and earth of Vitebsk, my birthplace, and of thousands of years of exile, find themselves mingled in the air and earth of Jerusalem?

"How could I have thought that not only my hands with their colors would direct me in my work, but that the poor hands of my parents and of others and still others, with their mute lips and their closed eyes, who gathered and whispered behind me, would direct me as if they also wished to take part in my life?

"I feel, too, as though the tragic and heroic resistance movement in the ghettos, and your war here in this country, are blended in my flowers and beasts and my fiery colors.

"The more our age refuses to see the full face of the universe and restricts itself to the sight of a tiny fraction of its skin, the more anxious I become when I consider the universe in its eternal rhythm, and the more I wish to oppose the general current.

"I know that the path of our life is eternal and short... I learned to travel this path with love rather than with hate.

"These thoughts occurred to me many years ago when I first stepped on Biblical ground, preparing to create etchings for the Bible. And they emboldened me to bring my modest gift to the Jewish people – to that Jewish people which always dreamt of Biblical love, of friendship and peace among all peoples; to that people which lived here thousands of years ago, among the other Semitic peoples. And this, which is today called religious art, I created while bearing in mind the great and ancient creations of the surrounding Semitic peoples.

"I saw the hills of Sodom and the Negev, out of whose defiles appear the shadows of our prophets in their yellowish garments, the color of dry bread. I heard their ancient words. Have they not truly and justly shown in their words how to behave on this earth and by what ideals to live? I draw hope and encouragement from thinking that my humble work will remain in their land, your land."

REUBEN

"Reuben, thou art my first-born, my might, and the first fruits of my strength; ...unstable as water..."

There is a sense of beginning, of the creation of the world, in this first window — symbolic of the birth of the first son.

This new world — the world of man — is given light by the rays of the sun shooting out in all directions. The sky and sea are in motion, flowing one into the other. Strong winged Chagall-like birds with unsheathed claws fly into the sun, in whose circles Chagall has spelled in Hebrew letters Jacob's blessing. Three birds fly in close formation through the center of the window; the middle bird, an eagle, with its crimson head and yellow beak, points up the strength and power promised by Jacob.

But Jacob knew Reuben's weaknesses, as well as his strengths. To show that he was "unstable," the window is awash with fish. They swim in all directions in a jewel-colored ocean of blues and purples and greens and reds. Each fish is wonderfully alive. You want to reach out

ראובן בכר
אתה כח
וראשית אונ
תר שאת

and touch their scales as they swim swiftly past you. Even on the still glass, they are in constant motion. Some of their jaws are wide open as if they were searching for food; but some with their open eyes seem to be weeping.

Flowers and ferns also live in Reuben's watery world. On the right is a child's flower in crimson and blue; it is the "mandrake," a flowering root that had healing powers, which the young Reuben brought as a gift from the fields to his mother. Right above the flowers is a green scene that has the quality of a dream. There is a green field with tiny grazing sheep whose soft fleece is etched in white. They seem to be walking toward a miniature pool inside their cool green dreamy world.

The whole window vibrates with a feeling of power and creativity. This is truly the beginning — the beginning of the story, the beginning of the family of Jacob.

SIMEON

"Simeon and Levi are brethren; weapons of violence their kinship... Cursed be their anger, for it was fierce... and their wrath, for it is cruel..."

Simeon follows immediately after Reuben on the east wall of the synagogue. In this window Chagall interprets Jacob's prophecy of "weapons of violence" as man's threat to destroy the earth and all those who are on it. A huge globe, in varying shades of lavenders and purples, whirling in space, dominates the window. It seems to be threatening the little houses of Vitebsk, which for Chagall are the houses of the world.

Across the entire bottom of the window, as if to emphasize the threat, is the first line of the prophecy "... and Levi are brethren, weapons of violence their kinship. Let my soul not come into their council..." Simeon's name is separated from the prophecy; it stands out alone in the small rose-quartz planet in the upper right. This globe on the right side and the smaller one on the left may stand for the divided tribes of Simeon and Levi as Jacob prophesied : "... I will divide them in Jacob, and scatter them in Israel."

Swirling around the globe are flying animals with outspread wings. A champing horse rides across the sky, his strength emphasized by the threatening green of his head and mane and the white smoke coming out of his nostrils. Yet even the fierceness of this prophecy is softened by Chagall's inner gentleness and sense of poetry. Just below the horse, swaying in the breeze, is a fairy tree with shining twinkling jeweled fruit.

This second window on the east wall between the blue of Reuben's and the yellow of Levi gives new insight into all the colors that are called blue. Here is an example of why Chagall is known as "the greatest colorist of our time."

LEVI

"They shall teach Jacob Thine ordinances; and Israel Thine Law; they shall put incense before Thee, and ... upon Thine altar."

Here is the Golden Rule in golden glass. Levi's window, in shimmering yellow, breathes forth an atmosphere of warmth and holiness. The Tablets of the Law dominate. Inside the iridescent lavender, blue, red and yellow of the Tablets, Chagall has put, instead of the Ten Commandments, Moses' blessing to the tribe of Levi.

The Star of David, in red, white and blue, with the Hebrew word Levi atop of it, is guarded by two charming birds. The dove on the left, in soft yellows and greens, like a dainty princess, wears a little white crown. Her companion has two tiny horns, like Michaelangelo's Moses, signifying wisdom.

In Chagall's bestiary, the animals also serve the Temple. Since human figures could not be used, two fantasy animals, holding a basket of fruit in rainbow colors, hover over the Tablets like a blessing. In ancient Israel the tribes brought their first fruits to the altar. In modern

לוי
ותורתך
MARC CHAGALL

Israel, children dressed in white with garlands of flowers in their hair sing and dance in a feast of thanksgiving for the first fruits.

Out of the tribe of Levi, the third son of Jacob, came the priests or Kohanim and the Levites, the guardians of the Temple. They became a sacred caste in ancient Israel, with the privilege of service at the altar. Moses, his brother Aaron, the High Priest, and his sister Miriam who guarded the infant Moses in the bulrushes in the river Nile, were Levites. Even today the Levites and the Kohanim play a special role in the synagogue service.

Flickering candlelight surrounds the altar on all sides like the candles which welcome the Sabbath Queen. The whole window, the last one on the east wall, is a paean of joy to the Sabbath; the day when God rested after He created the earth.

JUDAH

"Judah, thee shall thy brethren praise ... Thy father's sons shall bow down before thee. Judah is a lion's whelp... The sceptre shall not depart from Judah... His eyes shall be red with wine, and his teeth white with milk."

The south wall with the red windows — Judah and Zebulun — breathes fire!

In this powerful burning red window, the crown with Judah's name emblazoned on it in Hebrew carries Jacob's promise to Judah that his descendants would wield the sceptre and wear the crown. From his tribe would come the House of David with the great Kings of the Bible — David and Solomon. The prophet Isaiah and the leader Nehemiah also were Judah's descendants.

The Book of Kings tells us that at least once a year the Kings blessed the people, and thus below the crown we see hands outstretched in benediction.

Chagall's impish humor relieves the kingly splendor of velvety reds and purples. A sprightly lion with a curly tail gambols across the lower half of the window, carrying on his purple head the rooftops of Jerusalem, the city of David. Right under his nose, as if the lion were talking

in a medieval picture book, is Jacob's prophecy in Hebrew letters : "Thee shall thy brethren praise."

Judah and his brother Zebulun, following him on the west wall of the synagogue, are the only two windows in red glass. Chagall's genius and daring in the use of color placed these two windows side by side, sending a twin shaft of wine-red splendor into the synagogue.

Although Chagall signed each window, each signature is different. This window with Chagall's signature in the lower right corner is the only one in Hebrew letters, perhaps because this is the most mystic and prophetic of all the windows.

ZEBULUN

*"Zebulun shall dwell at the shore of the sea,
and he shall be a shore for ships..."*

A little dreamlike boat, that a child might paint in purple and green, sets out from the bottom of the window through the red sea into a purple setting sun.

Zebulun's tribe were the seafarers, bringing in goods from afar and trading with the ancient cities on the shores of the Mediterranean. Although Zebulun is the sixth-born son of Jacob, he is fifth in the order of the blessings, and therefore of the windows. The sages interpret this to mean that Jacob wanted Zebulun to engage in commerce and thus be able to support Issachar, who was to become the scholar of the family.

Chagall has created a magnificent and exciting design across the top of the window, simply by spelling out Zebulun's name in different colors of stained glass. Two large fish in shades of blue and lavender, swimming toward each other in the sky above the sun, represent the fruitfulness of the sea. It is Chagall's fantasy that the fish are

larger than the boats in which fish are caught. The fish are really the heroes of this window. For Chagall, fish and beasts and birds are all part of the fullness and goodness of life. He is depicting, in flaming red glass, Moses' blessing : "They shall suck the abundance of the seas, and the hidden treasures of the sand."

The descendants of Zebulun were also famous for the "treasures of the sand," glassmaking — the art Chagall now uses. They made their glass from the pure white sand they found in the ancient city of Acre north of Haifa. along the beaches of the Mediterranean.

Today, Israel, once again a nation engaged in fishing and commerce (and glassmaking), calls its seafaring organization the Zebulun Society.

Zebulun's little colored boat carries with it Chagall's faith in tomorrow, as it sails into a future of peace and brotherhood and love.

ISSACHAR

"Issachar is a large-boned ass, couching down between the sheepfolds... and the land that it was pleasant..."

This soft green window is in sharp contrast to the two companion red windows on the south wall. It is as if the little boat of neighboring Zebulun with its hope for peace sailed right into this peaceful pasture with its grazing sheep and its resting donkey.

Indeed "it was good ... and the land ... was pleasant." Here is the good earth. Here is the donkey with its blue head; its soft, almost feminine, eye; resting happily in the green field. Chagall's sense of fun shows again; a little bird perches on the haunches of the resting donkey. Above his head are grazing sheep and behind them a shepherd's staff.

The whole window is rich with the riches of the field : fruits and flowers, vines and wheat and barley. The tribe of Issachar was an agricultural tribe that toiled hard and was richly rewarded. It is recorded in the Bible that Issachar's people loved their land so much that they would

יששכר
חמר גרם
רבץ בין
המשפתים

not leave it to go to war and preferred therefore to pay double taxes.

This tribe was also known as the tribe of scholars because of the agreement with Zebulun, by which Zebulun, according to tradition, was to be the commercial tribe and Issachar was to be the scholarly tribe.

This is the only window completely framed within itself with ornamental scrollwork. The scrolls are actually the twining snakes, ancient symbol of fertility and wisdom. The snakes remind us too of the Biblical story of Moses' brother Aaron, whose rod turned into a snake when he threw it before Pharaoh.

The picture is dominated by two hands raised in blessing. The left hand is emerald green. The right hand, its fingers intertwined with the fingers of the left, is scarlet, holding up Issachar's blessing engraved in a white tent. "Rejoice," Moses said, "Zebulun in thy going out; and Issachar in thy tents."

DAN

"Dan shall judge his people, as one of the tribes of Israel. Dan shall be a serpent in the way, a horned snake in the path, that biteth the horse's heels, so that his rider falleth backward."

Dan is the Judge of Israel. Dan gave his name to the most northern city of ancient Palestine, the city of Dan — and travelers talked of going from Dan to Beersheba.

In Dan's window, the first on the west wall, the patch of yellow on the deep rich blue is like a window inside the window. Here is Chagall's genius! "Harmony in diversity" — one of his favorite quotes — takes on new meaning as we delight in the strong patch of yellow.

Chagall has followed the blessing quite literally in this window. The first sentence of the blessing, "Dan shall judge his people, as one of the tribes of Israel," swirls across the top of the window and around the left to the very bottom, where the word "Yisrael" stands out in beautiful Hebrew calligraphy. Right through the center of the window is a blue and green snake coiled around the base of a large candelabra. The snake with his flickering, darting tongue seems to be ready to spring

from the window, guarding the word "Yisrael" from the danger of the unsheathed sword and the horses seen in the right corner.

Three blue horses, in a ballet-like sequence, carry out the prophecy : "a serpent ... that biteth the horse's heels, so that his rider falleth backward."

Samson, the Judge, who avenged his people against the Philistines, was a descendant of Dan.

Standing like a human on its hind legs, a Chagall-animal in red is touching the flame in the middle of the candelabra with his left paw. With a long human right hand, the animal is holding aloft a rod — perhaps the rod of the scale of justice.

The two birds at the very top, the dove in red and blue with a pure white head, and the midnight-black raven, seem to represent light and darkness, day and night, good and evil. It is good and evil that Dan, the Judge, must weigh.

GAD

"Gad, a troop shall troop upon him; but he shall troop upon their heel."

A window of war! The deep green background is slashed through with the red of battle and blood! Troop upon troop engage in combat!

The clash of spears and shields and winged monsters can almost be heard.

This window, the second on the west wall, has a dream quality — a dream turned into a nightmare. Dragons and winged monsters with forked tongues out of the Inferno charge at you. A griffin with a red and white body and black wings stalks through the lower right carrying a shield and spears like an army on the march.

A broken earth splatters its blood over the wings of a fierce mythological bird, then down a straight shaft of light to a little familiar but blood-covered cow from Vitebsk.

Most of the animals are in motion, as if they are fleeing from danger — fleeing perhaps from the atom bomb.

והוא יגד

Chagall sometimes carries the symbols of one window into another. The human hand, holding a rod, which we saw at the top of Dan's window, is back again in miniature at the bottom of Gad's. It is the staff of justice — of man's knowledge of good and evil. It is this knowledge which makes man different from the beasts and fish and birds.

In the somber background, fortified city walls are bombarded by the rays of the enemies' shields. At the top right, the dove of peace is overturned, lying on his back with bloody head, and above, in the topmost circle, the name Gad stands out in solitary defiance.

The prophecy is fulfilled completely in the design of the window; destruction in the center and bottom and at the top, victory at war's end. Jacob had predicted that his son Gad would "triumph in the end." Although the enemy would fall upon him, he would turn defeat into victory.

ASHER

"As for Asher, his bread shall be fat, and he shall yield royal dainties." JACOB.

"Blessed be Asher above (the) sons... let him dip his foot in oil." MOSES.

Asher in Hebrew means happy or fortunate; and happiness and good fortune are reflected in his blessing. This soft green window, the last on the west wall, teems with a luxuriance of vines and olive trees and the richness of the produce of the earth.

The whole window is like a harvest basket. Here are the fruits of plenty and the jug of oil with a bird's head and a human eye.

Flying across the top of the window is a magnificent red bird carrying in his green beak the olive branch with its message of peace and the prosperity that comes with peace.

In the center there is a regal bird of many colors with a crown on his head — surrounded by the "royal dainties" fit for the king. Underneath his foot, in a swirling line of Hebrew letters, we find the first line of the blessing of Jacob, repeating, "his bread shall be fat, and he shall yield royal dainties."

אשר
שמנה לחמי והוא
תן מעדני מלך

The lower center is an oasis of quiet with the burning candelabra utilizing the oil to send forth its rays of light and hope for all who will listen to the message of peace set forth in this window.

Asher lived in a part of the Holy Land famous for its olive trees and the oil of the olives. Oil in Bible days was a precious possession. It was used for lighting, for cooking and for food itself. It was one of the most important exports of the country and was sold to all the neighboring peoples.

Playful animals remind us that this is Chagall's world too — a world of impish humor and love for even the smallest of God's creatures.

This is Chagall in a burst of colored glass singing, "Hallelujah! Let us praise the Lord."

NAPHTALI

"Naphtali is a hind let loose; he giveth goodly words."

The north wall of the synagogue has the window of the two favorite sons, Joseph and Benjamin, led by Naphtali.

It was Naphtali who ran swiftly to his father Jacob to tell him that Joseph was alive and a prince in Egypt. Naphtali, who brought the "goodly words" to Jacob, passed on to his sons and their sons the gift of oratory. The men of Naphtali were known for their eloquence.

The beautiful simplicity of Jacob's blessing finds reflection in the beautiful simplicity of this glorious yellow window. Here is the yellow gold of a Jerusalem sunset!

There are only two animals in this window, the gentle deer resting beneath the jeweled tree, and the eagle above him! This window fills us with a yearning to be quiet and to lose ourselves in the warmth and beauty of nature. Once again we see the memories of Vitebsk in the small crooked houses behind the head of the reclining hind.

נפתלי

Even the deer seems to be remembering the joy and the pain and the love.

The dominant color of the deer, even though it is red, it so muted that it too wins one to a restful mood. The other colors in varied shades of yellow, blue and green blend softly with the red.

The eagle, in sharp contrast to the deer, is in strong blues and reds with a yellow head and richly colored outstretched wings. This is a perfect example of the blending of the leading and the design.

While some windows are like an orchestra with wind and percussion instruments, this window is like a single song, a voice uplifted in a hymn of praise.

JOSEPH

"Joseph is a fruitful vine ... by a fountain; its branches run over the wall... The blessings of thy father... shall be on the head of Joseph..."

Joseph dominates the north wall as you step into the synagogue. The riches of the earth are spread before you. Golden wheat like the wheat in Pharaoh's dream! Grazing sheep ranging through the colors of the spectrum in yellow, blue, green and bronze glasses charm your senses.

"The branches run over the wall" reads the blessing in Genesis. The unusual vine with its red trunk and blue, green, yellow and red branches, expresses in a poetic way all the fruits of the earth in their varied colors. It recalls, too, the coat of many colors given to Joseph by his loving father Jacob.

Above the vine, holding a bow and arrow, there is a lavender and blue princely bird — as Joseph was a prince in Egypt. "The archers have dealt bitterly with him ... but his bow abode firm..."

At the top of the window are two human hands holding a ram's horn, or shofar. The shofar had many purposes

in Biblical days. In addition to calling the people to prayer, it was also blown to assemble them to listen to a message from the king. Today in modern Israel, the shofar is blown in the streets of all the cities and hamlets every Friday afternoon to announce the coming in of the Sabbath. When Pharaoh wished to honor Joseph, he let it be known throughout the land with the blowing of the shofar that Joseph was to be ruler of Egypt.

The name Joseph in Hebrew letters stands alone, encircled in shades of blue glass as Joseph stood alone and above his brothers.

There is a sense of tenderness and beauty and fruitfulness in the drenching golden colors of the sun.

BENJAMIN

"Benjamin is a wolf that raveneth; In the morning he devoureth the prey, and at even he divideth the spoil." JACOB.

"... The beloved of the Lord, he shall dwell in safety by Him; He will shield him all the day long, and between His shoulders will he dwell."

MOSES.

Benjamin, the last of the brothers, blazens forth in all the rich colors of the rainbow against the heavenly blue of the beginning of the world. In this one window are all the windows — all the sons — all the tribes! This window completely captures Chagall's childlike faith.

Here are the inhabitants of the earth — the plump lavender-tinted wolf with his blue and pink cat face, the little woolly lamb lying at his feet, the fish of fertility and the blue doves of peace nestling in a mauve bush. At the top of the window a flying blue and green bird seems to be talking to a pensive blue donkey with the face of the donkey in Issachar's window.

The golden city with its towers and roofs behind the wolf and the crooked houses in front of him could be all the cities of the world sheltering not only the family of Jacob, but the family of man.

In the upper left-hand corner a light-blue tree is seen — the tree of life, the tree of wisdom!

The tribe of Benjamin, "a wolf that raveneth," was noted for its excellent warriors in Biblical days. From Benjamin came the great heroes Saul and Jonathan.

In the window, the name Benjamin spelled out in Hebrew letters is divided, with three letters to the right of the shield and three to the left of the shield, as he "divideth the spoil." As his name is divided, so was his section of land on two sides of his brother's land.

Dominating the whole window is a galaxy of spinning worlds. This is Chagall's way of spelling out that man, through the tree of knowledge, has learned the mysteries of the world.

The story of the sons of Jacob is the story of all men's children.

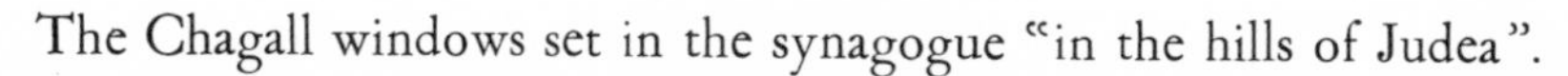

The Chagall windows set in the synagogue "in the hills of Judea".

ABOUT THE AUTHOR AND ARTIST

MARC CHAGALL – painter, illustrator, engraver, ceramist, water colorist – is considered by many to be a forerunner of the surrealists.

He studied at the Imperial School of Fine Arts, St. Petersburg, but his most important formative years were in 1910-1914, when he lived in Paris in close contact with the cubist painters and *avant-garde* poets. However, the Russian landscape and religious faith of his ancestors in the Jewish quarter of Vitebsk, where he was born, and where he later served as Commissar of Fine Arts, have inspired most of his work.

Between 1923 and 1941 the artist lived mainly in France, traveling also throughout Europe, Egypt, and the Near East. He resided in the United States and in Mexico from 1941 to 1947, but in 1947 Chagall returned to Europe, and in 1950 settled in Vence, in southern France.

Among his better-known works are *I and My Village* (1911; Museum of Modern Art, New York) and *The Rabbi of Vitebsk* (Art Institute, Chicago). He designed the sets for the ballets *Aleko* (1942) and *Firebird* (1945) and illustrated, among other books, Gogol's *Dead Souls* (1948), La Fontaine's *Fables* (1952), and the Bible (1956). In addition to the Jerusalem windows, he also designed the windows for the great Metz Cathedral.

MIRIAM FREUND is past President of Hadassah, and the woman who, with the architect of the Hadassah Hebrew University Medical Center in Jerusalem, first persuaded Marc Chagall to do the windows. Mrs. Freund received her B. A degree from Hunter College and her M. A. and Ph. D. degrees in American history from New York University. She is a well-known historian, author and lecturer. She has two sons and two grandchildren and makes her home in New York City.